New Teacher Notebook

New Teacher Notebook

*A Resource for New & International
Public School Teachers*

LaNora M. J. Foster, Ed.D.

XULON PRESS

Xulon Press
2301 Lucien Way #415
Maitland, FL 32751
407.339.4217
www.xulonpress.com

Paperback ISBN-13: 978-1-66287-007-1
Ebook ISBN-13: 978-1-66287-008-8

Preface

D r. Foster's passion for teacher recruitment and retention within her teaching career formed as she collected experiences as the new teacher within different schools, serving as department chairperson. After having a solid foundation of training and professional development during her student teaching and first four years of experience at Southside Middle School in Florence, SC, she realized that her initial experience of her career was not the norm. She learned that the level of mentor teacher training, access to a mentor teacher, and administrative and faculty support of new teachers to the profession and new to the school varied greatly. Serving as a mentor teacher to international teachers in two states highlighted the distinct challenges that these teachers conquered to satisfy survival needs and both acclimate to the new school environment and culture of the community. This epiphany stirred a passion within her to not only provide quality mentoring to teachers new to the profession, international teachers, alternatively certified teachers, and teachers new to the district/school/state, but to create a quick-reference resource applicable to teachers across the United States and beyond of the nuances within the majority of public schools.

New Teacher Notes' humble beginnings sprung from an inspiration to provide a series of over eighteen YouTube video clips, filled with valuable and relatable insight for the purpose of acclimating new teachers to the profession and to the new school community. This idea then grew to the establishment of the Facebook group, entitled the same, "New Teachers Notes," with a goal of becoming an online professional hub of support for first year or international teachers who are acclimating to the varied facets of effective teaching. This online community showcases the YouTube series of the same name, as well as posts inspirational quotes, professional articles, related videos, polls/surveys, and other valuable resources that seeks to address the needs of regular and special education, Pre-K through twelfth grade, fine art courses, and business or career courses. The membership of this online group has grown to extend across the United States and reached a few provinces in Canada.

"Tell me and I forget. Teach me and I remember. Involve me and I learn." ~Benjamin Franklin

Table of Contents

Chapter 1:

Preparing for the Interview

Education is a profession that has evolved over time, beginning primarily as a privilege of affluent males and later extending to affluent females. In the United States, it wasn't until after the Industrial Revolution that schools were created for middle- and lower-class students, typically housed in the town's centrally located church or some other designated building. Teachers also evolved from being an elite, well-educated man to a middle-class, never married female who had completed at least the eighth or ninth grade and successfully passed the "Teachers Exam." With that being said, there has been a fairly rapid progression in the qualifications required and certification process of public school teachers. Today, there are two tracks for certification: the traditional undergraduate and/or graduate-level teacher certification program or alternative certification programs. The traditional programs incorporate courses in pedagogy, curriculum, teaching techniques, and mentored internships. The alternative programs, such as Teach for America or Teachers of Tomorrow, incorporate fast-paced seminars in pedagogy, curriculum, and teaching techniques for a few weeks or months before they're placed in a position as classroom teacher, only to continue the training process on the weekends with mentors for up to a total of two to three years.

Whether teaching is your first or second career, preparing for an interview for a teaching career is important, as you will want to give a solid and assuring representation of yourself. Remember, you are representing yourself as an authority on the course content, as an effective instructor, and as a reliable and trustworthy member of the professional community. In the following sections, we will discuss preparing for interview questions and share a few examples of how to respond in a thorough but concise manner. Later, we will discuss giving that great first impression through presenting yourself in a professional manner.

When preparing for an interview for a public school teaching position, administrators will ask questions to determine your level of competence for the content area, your philosophy of education, your classroom management skills, communication skills, and likelihood to create and maintain professional expectations. Here are just three typical questions that administrators might ask of you during the interview:

1) **"What is your educational background?"**

This is your opportunity to share your college or university experience in relation to preparing for your future teaching position.

For example, if your undergraduate degree was cinematography, but you returned to university for a master's degree in chemistry and are now seeking an alternative teacher certification, briefly mention your undergraduate degree but spend most of your time stating your graduate degree and expound on how far you have progressed in the seminars or workshops for your alternative teacher certification.

It would be to your benefit, still using the scenario in the previous paragraph, to mention how your knowledge of cinematography will enable you to enrich the school's culture by assisting or creating a student organization that is focused on recorded plays or producing the school

2

news network. This may increase your candidate status significantly!

2) **Scenario Question: "You are in front of the class teaching when two students in the back of the room suddenly have a verbal altercation that is escalating by the second. How would you handle the situation?"**

This is the opportunity to express to them your ability to assess the level of concern, your ability to process the root of the issue, and your ability to quickly de-escalate the verbal altercation.

3) **"How would you deal with a situation where a student has just informed you that she has not turned in her homework all week because her parent/caregiver has been bedridden since coming home from surgery last week?"**

This is the opportunity for you to showcase your ability to express empathy and understanding to the student while opening communication with the parent. Discuss the use of school resources to assist the student by either offering tutoring services, after school care. You may also offer extended deadlines or collaborate with a school guidance counselor for possible community resources for the family.

Appropriate Interview Appearance

In preparing your outfit for the interview, you will need to take into consideration the surrounding community's cultural expectations for professional dress, as this may vary. As a rule of thumb, dress business casual. Make sure that your clothes are clean, neat, and wrinkle-free. Jewelry should be tastefully worn. Most communities' expectations for piercings and visible tattoos are still quite conservative, so be mindful of this and make decisions accordingly. Wearing sneakers to an interview may be appropriate if you have applied for a gym or coaching position. For other teaching positions, wearing shoes that align with business casual attire is the best choice. Perfume and cologne scents should also be tastefully muted. Remember that as a teacher, you are representing your school district, your principal, and your professional self to the parents within your community.

"Professional is not a label you give yourself–it's a description you hope others will apply to you." ~David Maister

NOTES

Chapter 2:

Summer Preparation

Communication with Administrators & Support Staff

Being a clear and thorough communicator is pertinent as a teacher and is a conscious relationship investment. This will pay in future dividends with building rapport and instructing your students, building trust with parents, and building long-term and positive relationships with administrators. So, what can you do during the summer to begin building relationships with administrators?

1) Send an email thanking them for the opportunity to work in their school. Also, offer to help with any preparations for the new school year (i.e., registration week, painting the hall/lockers, curriculum planning, etc.).

2) Plan an in-person visit at the half-way mark of the summer vacation. During this visit, ask your administrators if you can see your assigned classroom (if possible), collect your teacher's manuals, copy of the curricula, etc. This is also a great time to get to meet the entire administrative team, learning the locations of their offices, as well as the support staff (i.e., secretary, guidance counselors, and custodians). Remember, they are forming their first impressions of you as you are of them, so this is the time to show yourself as eager to learn, patient, willing to collaborate, and

mindful of how your work ethics affect their ability to effectively complete their work tasks!

3) Middle and high school teachers—express your genuine interest in assisting with one or more extracurricular activities or student organizations. If your participation during your first year is not possible due to a second job, family responsibilities, etc., be proactive by expressing this to the principal and let them know that you look forward to being active in this regard in the future.

Getting Acquainted with the Curriculum and Textbook

It is to your benefit to get acquainted with the textbook(s) and curriculum(a) that you will be following before the new school year begins.

1) Glance through these resources and jot down any questions to ask later.

2) Good resources to tap into are your district level instruction coordinator (don't be afraid to email, call, or set up an appointment), your school instructional coach, and/or your grade level teacher leader or department chairperson.

3) Be proactive in asking about any summer professional development that may give you additional insight to how to approach the curriculum and helpful instructional strategies. The more insight you have, the better! Some of these professional development workshops or seminars may be local and free. Others may be at the state, regional, or national level and require a fee payment, but most school districts will pay either half or the entire amount. Be sure to ask and fill out the necessary forms and submit in a timely manner!

Building your Curriculum Resources

Building your curriculum resources takes time. Thankfully, this time is often sped up with technology. However, the challenge is sifting through traditional and digital resources to find those that are most beneficial to your instructional strategies and your set of students' learning styles and needs each year. So, how can you be efficient in building these resources?

1) Ask your assigned mentor teacher and/or teacher buddy(ies) which resources they have found to be most effective in their classrooms.
2) Attend and participate in professional development that highlights and demonstrates curriculum resources. Be proactive in asking questions during professional development sessions … Don't be shy! Remember, if you increase your understanding of the resource and how it should be used in the classroom, the more likely you will use the resource properly and have success with it.
3) Intentionally dedicate at least one planning period each week throughout the school year to explore new curriculum resources or deepen your understanding of resources that you are currently using.

Classroom Set-up and Decorations

The ideal time in most administrators' perspective for teachers to come into the building to set up and decorate their classroom is a week or two before teachers are scheduled to report back to school. This is because each school varies in readiness for teachers because of the possibility of incomplete summer cleaning, floor waxing, painting, installment of large equipment, or delivery of furniture, to name just a few issues. Therefore, it is always a good idea for new teachers to call a week or so in advance of their arrival to ensure that their time and energy will be fruitful.

Remember to be patient and flexible during this process! Keep a running list of any broken, non-functioning, or absent items in your classroom. Contact the administrator and head custodian to ask what procedures you should follow to address these issues. Remember, this is your opportunity to make a first impression with these two people, so be polite, courteous, patient, and flexible!

Now, to actually set up and decorate your classroom! I recommend that you approach this process in "layers":

1) The location of the teacher's desk. Figure out the best location for your teacher's desk. Keep the following in mind:
   a) The desk should be close to the classroom door and easy for students and any classroom visitors to visually locate.
   b) The electrical and internet outlets may influence where a teacher's desk may be located.
   c) The teacher's desk should be positioned in a way that students can be adequately monitored at all times.

2) Arrange the students' desks or learning centers. Arrange students' desks or learning centers in a way that encourages various collaborative learning, as well as individual learning. Make sure that student seating offers clear and direct views to areas of focus (i.e. SMART Board, dry erase board, easel & chart pad, etc.Also ensure that there is adequate space for safe movement around student seating for students and any adults to pass through.

3) Designate areas in the classroom to display:
   a) Class rules, expectations, & consequences
   b) Lesson objectives (these may be displayed on PowerPoints or Google Slides instead)
   c) Homework
   d) Student work with feedback

e) Relative content displays (content and skill-based posters, content-related career choices)

f) School emergency information: school map, procedures, emergency folder, etc.

g) Hallway pass hangers

h) Bulletin board displays

i) Learning centers (elementary and/or middle school level)

j) Student assignment turn-in / pick-up station

4) Evaluate your classroom set up in regard to safety.

a) Can you and your students walk around safely? Where should students store their bookbags/items to ensure clear walking paths?

b) Can students exit the room quickly and safely?

c) Where is the best place for all students to go in the classroom in the case of a building intruder (i.e., away from any windows)? Is there enough room for all students to be out of sight? If there is not enough room, reconsider the placements of your students' desks or learning centers to accommodate this safety requirement.

5) Evaluate your classroom set up in regard to the special needs of your students. For example, if you have students with ADHD, you may want to make sure that there are places on the walls, floor, and ceiling that are "visual resting places" to reduce stimulation. Another example, if you have a student in a wheelchair, you may need a special desk that is tall and wide enough to accommodate a wheelchair, along with adequate room to maneuver the wheelchair around the classroom for collaborative learning.

SKETCH YOUR CLASSROOM SET-UP
(Individual Seating)

SKETCH YOUR CLASSROOM SET-UP

(Collaborative Seating)

Chapter 3:

Meeting Your Mentor & Building Your Professional Village

What should you expect from your assigned mentor teacher?

In a broad sweeping generalization, mentor teachers are usually teacher leaders who are naturally quite busy with many responsibilities within the school building and school district, as well as with their families and surrounding community. You have likely "hit the jackpot" with a person who is professionally well-connected, energetic, and has a wealth of professional knowledge, so take the opportunity to learn tidbits and tricks of the trade from them that would potentially take plenty of time and energy to learn on your own.

It is pertinent that you establish a plan with your mentor teacher for face-to-face meetings on a weekly basis for the first month before the school year begins. With that in mind, you should expect your mentor teacher to meet with you for thirty uninterrupted minutes per week to guide you through lesson reflections, troubleshoot classroom management issues, offer instructional strategies and resources, and just to offer encouragement. Do know that your face-to-face interactions after the first month of school may vary from once to twice a month, depending on both of your classroom locations and whether or not you two have common planning periods, as well as before and after school obligations.

However, emails and/or text messages may fill in any gaps with more flexible mentoring time that is needed.

What should you expect from your teacher buddy(ies)?

Your teacher buddy has a specific role that distinguishes him or her from just another teacher with a classroom nearby. This person serves in filling in the gap if and when your mentor teacher is unavailable. If you are fortunate, your mentor teacher may also serve as one of your teacher buddies if your classrooms are in close proximity to one another. This is not always the case, so we take the time to distinguish the separate role of teacher buddy. The following are reciprocal roles that you share with your teacher buddy:

1) **Cover Your Classroom for Short and Immediate Emergencies.** If you need to run to the restroom, administrator's office, make a quick call to a parent, or make extra copies, you should be able to depend on your teacher buddy to cover your classroom for five minutes or less. As this may disrupt instructional time of one or both classes, this benefit should be used only in cases of real emergency.

2) **Encouragement, Insight, or Clarification.** Your teacher buddy should be most helpful in offering encouragement or lending an empathetic ear after you've had a tough class period or incident. Also, when a long email is sent with complex or vague instructions, it is such a relief to check in with your teacher buddy to offer insight or clarification before acting. This is a time and energy saving technique, and it helps lower the daily stress level.

3) **Source of Instructional Resources.** Teacher buddies are a life saver when you run out of supplies (i.e., staples, calculators, working pencil sharpener, etc.). Be sure to be a good teacher buddy by pre-planning and stocking up on supplies, but should

the need to borrow arise, be sure to return the items and the favor promptly.

4) **Proactive Feedback.** It is important to choose a teacher buddy who is just as serious about your professional growth as they are of theirs. With that level of professional commitment, you can depend on your teacher buddy to give direct, constructive feedback on creative instructional strategies and classroom management issues.

"Intelligence plus character...that is the goal of true education."
~Dr. Martin L. King, Jr.

NOTES

Chapter 4:

Making the Most of the Professional Development Days/Week

The first days of work before the students' first day of school called "Professional Development Week", for most new teachers, can be quite exhilarating, as it is the beginning of the career that you have worked so hard to accomplish! It is quite normal to feel excited, confident, nervous, and so uncertain all at the same time. So, take a deep breath, hold it, then slowly release it. Everything will work itself out. Simply take it one step at a time and enjoy each moment. If you were fortunate enough to take care of the preliminary things, such as meeting the administrative team and support staff, setting up your classroom, and familiarizing yourself with your curriculum and textbook, you can relax a little, as a large portion of what needs to be done has been completed.

Meeting Faculty and Staff Members

Most new teachers are excited about embarking upon this professional journey and are full of energy about beginning the school year. You can expect that your principal will introduce you and all other new personnel to the building and to the rest of the faculty and staff on the first day, and you will suddenly realize that you need to not only learn your students' names quickly but also learn the names of your colleagues quickly. Prioritize learning the names of your administrative team, secretaries, hallway custodian, guidance counselor, attendance clerk, and grade level or department members first, as these are the persons with whom you will have early and consistent interactions. Make a point to stop by offices and classrooms and personally introduce yourself during less busy times to build rapport. Another way to get to know faculty and staff quickly is to make a point to sit with different people at department and faculty meetings throughout the professional development days. Showing your colleagues that you are friendly and willing to sincerely interact with different people will serve as a firm foundation to positive professional relationships.

Preparing your Syllabus

As the syllabus helps make the first impression of parents and students, it is important to have a clear, concise, thorough, and personable document to reduce the number of questions you may have to navigate later as the school year gets underway. When preparing your syllabus, you will need to include your classroom rules, expectations, and consequences, and collect information from the curriculum guide and textbook, incorporating school and district policies.

There are three people to contact for assistance with your syllabus: your mentor, grade level leader / department chairperson, and your teacher buddy. These three people can offer you valuable information about school district grading policies, curriculum pacing, etc. Make sure to communicate directly with these three people as you develop this syllabus, as doing so will save you time and energy in producing a cohesive and thorough document for inquiring parents and students.

Once you have your final draft prepared, it is a good idea to post your syllabus on your teacher webpage on the school website for the convenience of your parents and students. Also, send a copy of the syllabus to the grade level leader or department chairperson. Typically, I will also print some hard copies for parents on Open House night.

"The greatest sign of success for a teacher…is to be able to say, 'The children are now working as if I did not exist.'" ~Maria Montessori

NOTES

Chapter 5:

Preparing for Open House Night or Parent Night

M ost school principals are expecting the following from teachers on Open House Night or Parent Night:

1) Be on time and in place, whether that is at the general gathering place (i.e., cafeteria, library, or auditorium) for the initial presentation or at the door of your classroom, ready to receive parents and students.

2) Dress professionally! For most principals, the expectation is for teachers to give parents and students that first impression of being professional. Business-casual or semi-formal attire would be acceptable for such an occasion.

3) Have a parent log-in sign prepared. This is a great way to collect correct phone numbers and email addresses that may not be updated in the school's data system.

4) Be courteous, welcoming, and engaging to parents and students.

5) Keep your conversations engaging but brief. It is important for you to have the opportunity to engage with all visiting parents. If a parent wants an in-depth conversation, suggest scheduling a parent-teacher conference on a later date and time or communicate via email.

"Children must be taught how to think, not what to think."
~Margaret Mead

NOTES

Chapter 6:

Classroom Management

Establishing Rules, Expectations, & Consequences

Before tackling the nuts and bolts of creating your classroom rules, expectations, and consequences, let's take a moment to do some inner work! Teachers who teach in the same community as they were born and raised bring a unique and complex combination of background experiences, personalities, temperament, and world perceptions into the classroom. For example, if you were born and raised in a working class family, have a bubbly personality, are generally short-tempered, and see the world as a tough but a wondrous adventure, you might approach classroom management differently from a teacher who is from a more affluent family, is very quiet, focused, patient, and sees the world as a game that requires calm logic and strategy. Your energy or aura will be vastly different in some ways than the other teacher, and that sets the tone and approach toward classroom management. Neither teacher is necessarily destined for greatness or demise in regard to establishing the classroom culture. Now, take into consideration a teacher who begins teaching in a community that varies from his or her previous community. The disparity of perceptions and expectations requires even more awareness and flexibility.

The challenge for each teacher is to first be self-aware and routinely reflective as you conform your professional values and priorities with the expectations of your principal, parents, and students. Know that this is a continuous process, as expectations may evolve over time and depend on the school culture, so flexibility is needed. For example, you may personally prefer a relatively quiet and orderly classroom with students working individually or in pairs. However, there is a school initiative that requires teachers to implement more group collaboration and kinesthetic learning, which means students will need to get up, talk, and move around. You may panic at first in wondering how to maintain order and tranquility. You then decide to adapt to the new expectations and still maintain your personal preference by creating classroom procedures that will accommodate regular group collaboration and excited chatter and movement, but in a way that is systematic and orderly to ensure that your authority and class structure is not lost.

There is also a challenge in considering the unique combination of personalities, learning abilities, and social needs of students that change with each class, semester, or school year. One class may be naturally quiet, apt to listen, but slow to engage while much thought, energy, and consistency is required to quiet another class down each time to give their next set of directions. Both class dynamics may be a challenge for you to maintain engaging, high-quality, and positive learning environments throughout the semester or school year, but doing so builds and strengthens your classroom management skills.

Thankfully, there is no need to reinvent the wheel of classroom expectations and consequences! Just keep the following concept in mind as you create your class culture:

1) Take note of classroom rules of other teachers to see which rules resonate with the classroom culture you desire to create.
2) Keep your classroom rules to ten or fewer. The more concise your rules are, the more likely your students will be able to remember them!
3) Use positive words within your classroom rules to increase the likelihood of yielding positive results. Compare the wording: Example: Don't come to class late!

Example: Be prompt to class!

4) Include clear consequences for class rule infractions. This list should be short, with just three to five steps. Most schools and school districts have an established policy for consequences to ensure consistency. Defer to your school/district's policy.

Effective Daily Classroom Management Techniques

Once you have created and taught your classroom expectations, rules, and consequences, you are ready to commence with the curriculum with vigor! In regard to classroom management, know that you are most often the winner if you remain proactive. Students are more likely to lose focus and get off-track whenever they feel unseen and are not actively engaged in the lesson. Keeping this in mind, use proximity, redirection, and proactive communication, which goes a long way in eliminating those feelings and greatly reduces the likelihood of disengagement.

Let's focus on proximity first. Students are most likely to remain focused if they know that you can see them, might walk over to their desk, or can see what they are doing at any given time during class. This is a fantastic deterrent for most students. When you are deciding how to set up student desks in different groupings, you should consider the ease with which you can navigate around your classroom. There should not be any place in your classroom that you avoid going over to because of the awkwardness of walking around. That being said, make it a habit to move around your classroom regularly while you are giving instruction and while students are working independently. Also make sure that you can easily see each student from your teacher desk as well.

Creating lessons that are engaging for students is key to reducing classroom management issues. Students should be engaged from the moment they enter the classroom (i.e., bell ringer, reading time, etc.) until the end of the lesson (i.e., reflection, quiz, parking lot questions, etc.). Take into consideration the grade level, attention span, learning styles, and level of rigor required for each class. For example, to keep typical kindergarten students engaged, you will likely need to divide class time between group time and learning station time in fifteen to twenty-minute intervals with plenty of visual, vocal, and kinesthetic aids to encourage learning to take place. For middle or high school students who have forty-five to ninety minutes within each class, the lesson needs to be divided into fifteen to thirty-minute segments for instruction, modeling, group collaboration and/or individual practice. This lesson structure typically accommodates visual, auditory, and kinesthetic learners and ensures interaction and focus throughout the lesson.

Redirecting students when they are off task is the third proactive technique to discuss. On the occasion that a student is distracted by someone or something, be quick to notice their lack of focus, and use a firm but empathetic tone that lets the student know "I know it may be hard to focus right now, but this is important, and I care about your success." A repeated reminder for the same student during the same lesson should progress with a firmer tone. Should you need to redirect the student more than twice in one class period, a follow-up, quick one-on-one conversation at the end of class is a good idea to see what is causing the lack of focus. This may be a case of the student just having a bad day and may not need further action. However, if their inability to focus is due to an ongoing issue, such as dealing with parents' divorce, grief, depression, etc., you may need to take further action, such as contacting their parents/caregivers or guidance counselor for additional support.

Proactive communication is a crucial tool for the teacher to minimize confusion and downtime, which often leads to students' mischievous behavior. This entails careful lesson planning and mindful communication through intentional verbal cues. Being intentional in your communication includes planning, reflection, consistent awareness, and effective communication.

Example:

As students walk into class, you inform them of their first task: "Good morning, Myla! Your bell ringer assignment is on the SMART Board. You will need to take out your laptop and textbook."

Example:

After teaching the lesson, you tell them about and then model their group assignment, but also tell them explicitly what they are to do once their group is finished: "Okay, what questions may you have about the group assignment? [Give students "think time" for five seconds] Okay, when your group finishes, you are to return to your individual seats and complete the graphic organizer for the next lesson. You will have until the end of class to complete it. I will have a sample of it posted on the Smart Board and will be walking around to assist you, should you have questions. Any questions? Okay, you may begin in your groups."

Documentation of Classroom Behaviors

Good classroom management entails daily reflection and documentation of any classroom behaviors that will potentially endanger the learning environment that you are cultivating. Keeping good and consistent documentation is beneficial in that you are able to detect patterns of behavior, pinpoint actual dates that behaviors occurred, and communicate this information to parents/caregivers, administrators, and guidance counselors as needed. This documentation also protects you as a professional, who may be called upon to submit an affidavit legal document or testify in court, and gives validity to your classroom management decisions in parent or administrative conferences.

Many school districts have invested in various online behavioral database programs where student behavior can be documented and accessible by school personnel (i.e., administrators, guidance counselors, and teachers). Even disciplinary referrals can be submitted on some of these programs. Many teachers keep a designated physical notebook or an online spreadsheet on which they document negative student behaviors.

Wherever you choose to consistently document these negative behaviors, be sure to also consistently document contact with parents or caregivers. Indicate whether the contact was via phone, email, text message, letter, conference, or that you chatted with them at the local grocery store about their student's behaviors.

This documentation should be concise, thorough, and without personal opinion. You should include the date and the approximate time. Here are a few examples of such behavioral documentations:

Example #1:
8/17/2022 @ ~ 9:15 a.m. – Sandy M. blurted out in the middle of silent reading time, "I hate school!" and then got up from her seat, walked to the bookcase, and slammed the book on the shelf. She stomped back to her desk and drummed loudly on her desk with her pencil. She did not respond to several verbal cues that she should be reading, to choose another book she likes, and to not make noise. She also would not leave when directed to go for a time-out in Mrs. Smith class next door.

Example #2:
3/10/2023 @ ~12:45 p.m. – Kevin G. hit another student with his laptop after a verbal altercation with that student. Kevin did not respond to verbal warnings and directives to stop talking and move away from the other student. According to Kevin and the surrounding students, the other student made an offensive statement to Kevin, which began the verbal altercation. The other student who was hit denied making an offensive statement.

Importance of Fairness and Consistency

Building a high emotional intelligence quotient (or the innate or acquired ability to detect a person's emotions, needs, thoughts, or intentions) goes a long way in maintaining a peaceful, vibrant learning environment for students and a rewarding working environment for you, the teacher. The main components of building rapport, trust, and respect from your students are fairness and consistency in classroom management as you interact with students for both positive and negative behavior. Many of us can share stories of feeling hurt from unfair treatment or inconsistency with authority figures who did not follow established policies. The best way to approach implementing fairness and consistency is to make these behaviors intentional and a priority on a daily basis. This involves self-awareness, command of your own emotions, active listening to your students, a <u>healthy</u> dose of empathy, willingness to admit mistakes and apologize to students, and daily reflection for future improvement.

The more aware you are of who you are as a person, which entails your strengths and weaknesses of your personality as well as understanding how your life experiences affect your worldview and daily behaviors, the better you will be able to navigate interactions with students who come with their own personalities and set of life experiences. Identifying strengths and weaknesses of your personality begins with first identifying your personality type from various assessments. One of the most common personality assessments, and arguably one of the most accurate, is the Myers-Briggs Personality Indicator[1].

One of the hardest challenges for many people is to get and stay in tune with their emotions at all times and then control that emotion in a way that will yield the best outcome for you and your relationship with yours. As a professional, you are recognized first as being human, but you will also be expected to hone this skill to the proficiency-level over time to best serve students, parents/caregivers, and the school community. Again, this is a challenge for most people on a "good day," and even more so on days when things are not falling into place, so it is important to be intentional in this every day.

---

[1] www.16personalities.com

Being an active listener of your students means to balance your role as an authority figure and instructional leader with being a role model and mentor to your students. When students know that you are indeed listening to them, their struggles, their fears, concerns, and need for attention and acceptance, they are more likely to comply with your instruction and direction.

Having a healthy dose of empathy goes hand in hand with being an active listener. When you hear what your students are saying to you verbally and nonverbally, showing that you care makes students feel heard, seen, and emotionally safe. This is not the same as giving into or allowing students to have their way most of the time. You must be willing as an adult and authority figure to admit that you make mistakes and that you understand that apologizing to students is just as important to them as it is for you to receive an apology from someone who has offended you. All of these components help to establish an environment of respect and reciprocity between students and the teacher, based on the need for both to develop a positive, long-term relationship in the learning process.

Lastly, developing the daily habit of reflecting over the day's lessons and events is a great way to keep your professional ego in check, even on days that seem so hectic and unpredictable. Taking just a few moments at the end of your workday to reflect, assess, and identify ways to improve or things to correct for the next day can make a world of difference. Students definitely notice your efforts to improve your craft, your verbal delivery, and your relationship with them, and they are likely to respond positively and with renewed commitment to improve their behaviors as well.

Parent/Guardian Communication

One of the most daunting aspects of the teaching profession for new teachers is developing positive relationships with the parents or guardians of your students. Be aware that you will most likely have a mixture of personalities, backgrounds, and value systems to navigate, just as you have with your students. Therefore, it's important to be sincere, intentional, flexible, and self-aware as you make the first impressions of the school year. Here are a few suggestions:

1) **Set up a Teacher Webpage** – If your school offers it, set up your teacher webpage on the school website. Include a brief greeting to parents and students that share your professional background, educational philosophy, and expectation for a great school year. This is also a great place to insert your class syllabi, grading scale, and contact information for parents' convenience. Most principals and school superintendents prefer any self-images on teacher pages to be a professional picture with either your classroom or a neutral wall as a background (i.e., skip the bathing suits, vacations, glamorous, and family pictures, etc.). It is always a good idea to check with the school webmaster to get approval of pictures being uploaded, especially if you are not sure of the appropriateness of your picture.

2) **Open House / Family Night** – Be positive and engaging with parents/guardians, but keep the conversations light and brief, as you want to acknowledge everyone attending. It is a good idea to have a repeating slide presentation on display, a brochure, displayed student work, or copies of your syllabi available for parents and guardians to see or pick up.

3) **Emails, Texts, and Calls** – Start the school year off by approaching parents and guardians with positive messages about their students via emails, text messages, or phone calls within the first two to three weeks! If early negative behaviors are emerging, don't hesitate to make those calls as well.

4) **Parent/Caregiver Conferences** – Whether the conference is initiated by the parent/guardian or by yourself, be sure to give positive vibes by avoiding closed body language (i.e., crossed arms, stern facial expressions, etc.). When communicating any negative behavior or learning issues of a student, follow this conference formula:

a) **Greet the parent or guardian.** Thank them for their time and interest.
   Example: "Good morning, Mr. Jensen. I'm glad that you were able to meet with me on such short notice."

b) **Share some positive characteristics or behavior of the student** that you've noticed. *Example*: "Samantha is such a helpful person! Just last week, she was quick to help another student who'd dropped their bookbag with all of the books and papers falling out. And just yesterday, she lent one of her pencils to a student who'd lost theirs. And she does this before anyone asks for help."

c) **Address the concern or issue or concern** without imposing personal opinion of the student's character, then allow time for questions from the parent or guardian. *Example*: "Mr. Jensen, this morning Samantha turned in a project, which was due today. I noticed that the original name was crossed out with a Sharpie marker and Samantha's name was written above it. When I asked Samantha about this after class, she admitted that the project was another student's. She said that she'd left hers at home this morning, and when she saw this project was left on the bus, she took it and turned it in as hers."

d) **Clearly state the consequences** for the behavior (current and future). Remind the parent of the consequences of breaking the class rule or school/district infraction outlined in your class rules or school district's discipline code book. *Example*: "Mr. Jensen, Samantha is aware that passing someone else's work off as her own is an infraction of the school district's policy and can result in a zero for her grade on the assignment and parent notification for the first offense. I reminded her that a second offense will result in a zero and a discipline referral."

e) **Clearly state how the parent or guardian can support you.** Example: "Mr. Jensen, I would really appreciate it if you would have a conversation with Samantha about this and make sure that she understands how serious it is to take credit for someone else's work."

f) **Close the conference with a positive and sincere statement about the student**. Example: "Thank you again for agreeing to meet with me. Samantha made the wrong choice this morning, but I expect that she will continue to do well academically and be the loving person that she is! I'm sure the next report to you will be stellar!"

Building a Solid Foundation for Positive Classroom Management in the First Two Weeks

Most new teachers have an innate urge to just get started with the curriculum and get students engaged in the learning process, so there is a sense of rush to cover school and classroom rules and policies. Unfortunately, if a teacher does just that, it will undoubtedly yield a series of classroom management issues, and the teacher will become frustrated, overwhelmed, disillusioned, and discouraged in just a matter of four to six weeks.

First, let's acknowledge the importance of getting students started with the learning process. Yes, it's important to not stall to the point of getting behind with the curriculum pacing guide. However, it is important to understand that you must allow for establishing expectations and procedures to a classful of human beings with a unique combination of personalities, background experiences, and needs of which you are not fully aware. In the same token, students are finding themselves in a classroom with a different combination of their peers than what they are used to. They may be familiar with some or most of their peers, but as you are a new teacher to the building, they see you (i.e., your personality, your expectations, your temperament, etc.) as the biggest mystery within the four walls of their classroom. With this acknowledgement, it behooves you to take a methodical approach to identifying the mechanisms of the learning environment that you will be cultivating within your classroom.

The needs of students in every grade level, different learning abilities, and class schedule times will vary. However, the pacing of building rapport, community, and structure within your classroom should closely resemble the following pattern:

Day One:

- Seating Chart – Immediately establish a sense of structure by preparing a seating arrangement for students but inform them that there will be regular collaborative settings with others daily.
- Introductions/Ice Breakers – This activity is an important step toward illuminating the personalities, the interests, and temperament of your students. This also gives you an opportunity to dispel some of the mystery surrounding you as a human and teacher and to get students out of their desks to expel some of their nervous energy and help them to stay attentive while you are covering the next first day of school topics.
- School/District Procedures & Policies – It is a great idea to make this section of time interactive and engaging (i.e., class discussion, Q&A, create a class board game, etc.). Choose the most urgent procedures and policies for the first day (i.e., emergency procedures, lunch schedule and procedures, etc.).
- Classroom Rules/Expectations & Consequences – Cover these thoroughly and give some relatable examples to answer questions they may have (including what this behavior looks/sounds like and what this behavior does not look/sounds like).
- Choose to cover the most urgent information for the first day during homeroom or first period (i.e., lunch time, recess time, homeroom location and times, locker combinations, etc.).
- Content Activity – Have students engage in a short (five to fifteen minutes) and engaging activity that involves subject matter. This activity may be a review of skills or information from a previous grade or pre-requisite course.

- Closure – Facilitate a verbal recap and have students write a short reflection or give a short, non-graded quiz, etc.

Day Two:
- Introduce any new students and revamp seating arrangements if necessary.
- Conduct a short, fun, and engaging activity that involves subject matter–Use this opportunity to teach students class expectations and procedures as they collaborate, having a brief class discussion about them before students are allowed to move into collaborative groups.
- School/District Procedures & Policies–Briefly review the previous day's information before covering new material (i.e., library/hallway passes, etc.)
- Review the Classroom Rules/Expectations & Consequences briefly before covering class procedures
- Begin covering class procedures–(i.e. class and homework Turn-in/Pick-up Stations; entering and leaving classroom; raise hand before speaking; and roles within groups)
- Content Area Collaborative Activity with emphasis on practicing desired classroom behaviors

Days Three-Five:
Slowly begin the curriculum with much emphasis on students correctly following class rules, behavior expectations, and procedures. Give ample individual and collective feedback throughout the class period. Be sure to use positive reinforcement and assure students that they are progressing in the positive direction. Be positive, but firm in redirecting students who are exhibiting negative behaviors. It's also a good idea to send parents an email or text message for positive behaviors and contact parents of students who are exhibiting negative behaviors. Remember: Be positive, firm, and consistent!

Chapter 7

Building Relationships with Support Staff

As you are acclimating yourself with the faculty and staff, it is a good idea to intentionally make a good impression with those who will be serving you as your first line of support on a daily basis. The school secretaries are some of the busiest people within the building, as they are delegated to greet visitors, serve as liaison between and for administrators, answer the school's main phone line, and help troubleshoot teacher emergencies, to name just a few responsibilities. Needless to say, it's important that you maintain a good rapport with the secretaries, as they have a wealth of information and resources to impart. Here are a few points to remember when interacting with school secretaries:

1) **Be proactive!** Communicate <u>early</u>, if at all possible, if you know that you will be absent from work or if there is a problem that needs to be addressed immediately.

2) **Be concise but thorough.** Relay information so that good decisions can be made efficiently.

3) **Show appreciation!** This may be something as simple as a smile, "Thank you," or an occasional gift certificate for a free cup of coffee.

4) **Send an email** if the issue is not an absolute emergency, then follow up later if there is no response in an hour or two.

5) **Show growth in your resourcefulness!** As you learn the locations, people, and roles, be sure to troubleshoot your own dilemmas whenever possible.

Custodians are another invaluable resource within each school building. They know the location of every storage closet, have the keys to every exterior and interior door, know the ins and outs of each restroom, and are one of the first to be called whenever there is a spill or emergency involving bodily fluids. Here are a few points to remember when interacting with custodians:

1) **Formally introduce yourself!** Use good body cues (i.e., eye contact, smile, posture, respectful voice tones).

2) **Be friendly!** Most custodians are people persons! Share a few things about yourself. Custodians are quite observant, and they notice new people on campus right away. They are often naturally curious about your personality and level of tidiness, as well as your personal interests.

3) **Be proactive and considerate!** Contact a custodian in advance if you need large trash bags for cleanup, more paper towels, etc., as they have quite a full daily routine that will be interrupted if there is an emergency.

4) **Tidy your classroom!** Clean up your classroom and throw personal trash away properly by the end of each class period with your students. Most custodians are responsible for sweeping/vacuuming and emptying trash cans in twenty or more classrooms and offices each day, not to mention the restrooms. Routinely keeping a clean, neat classroom goes a long way when asking custodians to go the extra mile for a future favor.

5) **Show appreciation!** This may be something as simple as a smile, "Thank you," or an occasional gift certificate for a free cup of coffee.

Administrators serve in multiple roles as the overseers of the school building's maintenance, bus transportation, student discipline, teacher attendance, school safety, parent and community liaison, recruitment and retention, curriculum and instruction, special education accommodations, and after-school activities. Every day and every hour is different and equally demanding in a variety of ways. Keeping this in mind, it is important that you make an effort to create and maintain open and clear communication with administration at all times. Here are a few points to remember when interacting with administrators:

1) **Follow school rules and procedures!** Those rules and procedures are in place for a reason, and you make the jobs of administrators that much easier when you are in alignment. In the case when you need to make an exception, be sure to explicitly communicate the reason to them.

2) **Be proactive!** If there is an issue of school safety or major classroom disruption or emergency, contact them without any hesitation.

3) **Send an email!** If you have a non-emergency question or concern, send members of the administrative team an email, then follow-up if there is not a response within a few hours or so.

4) **Interact with integrity and professionalism!** Administrators must make major decisions regularly, based on the information that they gather. It's important to communicate with integrity at all times. Being consistently professional in your interactions also helps to build their trust in you over time as an employee as well (i.e. report to work on time, dress appropriately, have appropriate conversations, turn in documentation and lesson times on time, etc.)

5) **Be flexible!** Tough decisions are constantly being made. It is important to create a balance between voicing your truth and understanding that administrators are dealing with unchangeable circumstances. So your understanding and willingness to be flexible goes a long way in building a rapport with the administrative team.

6) **Show appreciation!** This may be something as simple as a smile or an email just to say thank you.

Guidance counselors were once the ones who only took care of student permanent files, student schedules, standardized testing, college preparations, and some student behavior intervention. Today, counselors are doing all of those things plus a much heavier load of counseling students dealing with domestic trauma, violence, and severe social and emotional needs. Here are some points for building a solid working experience with guidance counselors:

1) **Be flexible and patient!** Student schedules take time to adjust at the beginning of the school year or semester. Follow the procedures the guidance team communicates to the faculty about accepting new students and email the guidance team and be patient. Most adjustments are usually made no later than the second week of school.
2) **Be proactive!** If you see or hear evidence of a student in an abusive situation, notify an administrative and guidance counselor immediately. If there is a non-emergency, send an email and follow-up in a few hours or the next school day if needed.
3) **Be discreet!** Be mindful of sending emails with personal student information or concerns and the language that is used, as these emails may be subpoenaed by lawyers or the court at any given time.
4) **Show appreciation!** This may be something as simple as a smile or an email just to say thank you for their support.

"Knowing your *why* and where we are in the process helps to build our levels of **patience**, **hope**, and therefore **endurance!**"
~ Dr. LaNora M. J. Foster

NOTES

Chapter 8:

Self-Care

Keeping our physical bodies healthy as teachers means taking a few extra steps of care, as we are immersed daily in a cesspool of bacteria, viruses, and germs. It is the nature of what this career entails. Since the COVID-19 pandemic, I believe that a heightened awareness of transmissible viruses has brought about some changes that may be permanent, such as the wearing of face masks within the school building, especially during the seasons that yield high respiratory infections within the community. Both teachers and students are encouraged to wash their hands and/or use hand sanitizer more often as a way to prevent the spreading of infection. Also, many are being more mindful of encroaching upon another person's personal space and providing less congested seating options.

With teaching being a naturally stressful job at times, it is advisable to incorporate regular physical exercise. This could involve yoga, walking, jogging, kickboxing, or Zumba, to name a few. While some teachers may prefer to do this individually, fitting exercise whenever they can within their hectic and inconsistent schedules, other teachers may find that corporate exercise truly helps them to make exercise a priority and a habit. Check with your local education association to see which local gyms offer gym membership discounts for teachers, and rally a few of your colleagues to join you. Also, some school leaders have become proactive in initiating regular or seasonal physical health challenges, such as breast cancer and heart health awareness walk challenges or just a random "get fit" challenges to rally teacher morale and health during a stressful time of the school year. In any case, get out there and get moving so that there will be a healthier, happier teacher in front of the classroom, which trickles positive dividends to students.

Getting adequate sleep is all important as a teacher. Teachers are expected to be on their A-game every day, from the moment they enter the building until they leave at the end of the day. There's no telling what situation(s) (and for what length of time) the instructional leaders or adults within the school building may face on any given day. Being sleep deprived will place you at a significant disadvantage in thinking with clarity or responding to an emergency or pivotal scenario. In a utopian society, every teacher would arrive at work with eight to ten hours of deep, restful sleep. However, with many teachers being parents of babies and small children, primary caregivers of elderly parents, having second and third jobs, or just dealing with varying levels of stress for any of life's challenges, some teachers feel fortunate to have at least five to six hours of sleep. Adults require approximately seven to eight hours of sleep each night for optimal job performance.

Serving in the classroom as the instructional leader, emergency supervisor, student mentor, counselor, encourager, conflict mediator, and more can and will eventually take its toll on you emotionally, as well as impact your mental health at times. You should be mindful to guard your mental health with as much diligence as you do your physical health. When mental health is discussed, many have the perception that mental health is dealing with major psychological disorders, such bipolar disorder or schizophrenia, and therefore dismiss others, such as the "common colds" of psychological disorders, such as depression, anxiety, and several others. Mental illness can be developed by anyone just as anyone can contract a physical illness. Just as you have to watch your diet, water intake, exercise, and protect yourself from germs, etc., you should be as diligent in setting boundaries, maintaining a sense of work/life balance, and choose to be positive, as well as seek positive modes of relief from negative stress.

Each teacher's work schedule may vary according to grade level, needs of their students, and teacher duties, along with the hectic personal schedules that vary according to your particular stage of life and the combination of challenges that life may have presented to you (i.e., pregnancy, babies and small children, supporting children's after-school activities, purchasing a home, moving, spousal responsibility, single-parenting, divorce, elderly parents, personal illness, etc.). One teacher once made the statement, "I feel like I am always on the go and life doesn't slow down. If I have a personal crisis, I'm still expected to perform at a high level. There is little room for slowing down and taking care of myself or my family." Because this sentiment is quite common among teachers, most of whom are very conscientious, many chronically place themselves last on the list. This culture of self-sacrifice seems to be ingrained within the teaching career.

Unfortunately, this culture of self-sacrifice has quietly eroded the morale of teachers, as many have quietly suffered from burnout and eventually change professions or choose early retirement. The teacher shortage has alerted educational leaders of this reality, and many school districts have become more proactive to combat this issue.

There are several things that you can do personally to prevent or cope with episodes of burnouts, should you find yourself experiencing the symptoms.

1) **Avoid overextending yourself.** Assess your personal obligations before the school year begins and decide to what extent you will be able to reasonably accept additional work responsibilities and obligations beyond your assigned teacher duties. Have a candid conversation with your principal about your availability and express your willingness to volunteer or participate more in the future when your situation changes for the better, then stick to what you have assessed to be doable.

2) **Reserve quiet time.** This may mean that you come to work fifteen to thirty minutes earlier or stay fifteen to thirty minutes later than

is required, or both. Honoring your need to be in a quiet place mentally and reflect or just relax.

3) **Maintain work-life balance.** Decide to only allow yourself to take work home only once or twice a week. Allow yourself to be fully attentive to your family and friends, or just treat yourself to something that you really enjoy doing.

4) **Invest in yourself.** Everyone needs "down time," including teachers. Cultivate a hobby, read a professional or self-help book, or enroll in a course that interests you.

5) **Build your professional village.** This includes mentor teachers, teacher buddies, and other colleagues who are positive, knowledgeable, and encouraging.

Despite our efforts, at times, the responsibilities and challenges of teaching and life can sometimes be overwhelming, and symptoms of burnout may be quickly manifested. Many times, teachers shrug and attribute the first few symptoms to various life factors and may not become fully aware of what is transpiring until they are totally overwhelmed. Teacher burnout occurs when the feeling of extreme mental exhaustion is experienced over a prolonged period of time. This feeling often affects a teacher's level of functionality and productivity. The following are typical symptoms of teacher burn-out:

1) Irritability
2) A sense of dread and cynicism about your professional responsibilities
3) Depersonalization of students, parents, administrators, etc.
4) Panic attacks or noticeable nervousness
5) Insomnia
6) Drastic change in weight (loss or gain)
7) Feeling both physical and mental exhaustion
8) Lack of confidence of effectiveness in the classroom

Once you have self-awareness and recognize that you are indeed feeling burnout, there are several things that you can do to alleviate the symptoms over time. As with any physical illness, it will take intentional coping methods and time for symptoms to significantly improve, so be easy on yourself as you're recovering emotionally and mentally. The following are suggestions to alleviate teacher burnout over a period of time:

1) Be intentional in making meditation and reflection a daily habit.
2) Be intentional in incorporating exercise or physical activity to relieve stress.
3) Lean on your professional village for support.
4) Establish and maintain work-life balance.
5) Read and listen to inspirational books and videos.

"Self-care is not about self-indulgence.
It's about self-preservation."
~ Audrey Lorde

NOTES

Chapter 9:

Coping with Culture Shock

Entering the classroom for the first time for any new teacher can undoubtedly be exciting and overwhelming as you assess and reassess your to-do and reminder list, then add the aspect of interacting with and instructing students from a community that is different from the one that you experienced during your student experience. Some may assume: "Students are pretty much the same no matter which corner of the country or world you encounter them." While that statement may hold some truths, cultural nuances do exist, and try as hard as you might, you're likely to stumble across a few of those cultural nuances at less than convenient and discreet times. These moments may cause you to lose focus, become utterly befuddled, and lose precious time of instruction and/or opportunities for building rapport with students and parents alike.

One of the first things to absorb, ideally before the school year begins, is an understanding of the values of that community. For example, if the community is agricultural, the value system may be centered around collectivism, a sense of obligation to the family, farm, and surrounding farming community. Time for proper care of farm animals or plants may aggressively rival the importance of time spent on your social studies homework assignment. Therefore, parents may allow their student to remain home from school because a new calf or goat was born in the wee hours of the morning and the student was needed to help that process. Another example would be if your teaching position is in a metropolitan city where there is an NFL team, and support of the team is taken quite seriously. Many parents may sign out their students to attend an opening game that is played at home, and tailgating starts at 2 p.m.; never mind the fact that you scheduled a biology test for that day two weeks ago. Understanding the values and the behaviors that are the norm within the community are helpful in making your lessons and teaching examples relevant and building rapport with community members easier. Your agreement with those values are irrelevant when it comes to being an effective teacher within that community.

Learning the jargon and colloquialisms that are unique to the community is also helpful. An experience comes to mind when I began teaching at a charter alternative high school in Anacostia, Southeast Washington, D.C. The enrolled students were all mandated to attend this charter school by the D.C. Juvenile Court System after the students' behavioral or attendance issues made it evident that a regular school setting was not adequately meeting their unique needs. Now, you must understand that all of these students had multiple stories of negative and even traumatic interactions with law enforcement, and neighborhood gangs were well established and served as an ongoing menace to the community for generations. The name of the game for these students was to create and maintain the facade of a tough exterior, but inside, they struggled to nurture their embattled younger self and yearned for acceptance and love from the adults within the building. One way to maintain a tough facade for these students was to create sentences using curse words for the noun, verb, and predicate whenever one felt one's ego or physical self was being threatened. This behavior was repeated often enough, along with physical bluffing and perhaps one or two actual fights until one would get evidence of gaining respect and acceptance from their peers. There were also code words that were used that everyone in the community knew but would fly over the heads of any outsiders. One of those such words was "steal/stole." One morning, as I was performing a mandatory "pat-down" of the female students for any illegal substances or weapons, one young lady stood a few inches away from me, staring me down with a piercing glare, and her face set in a way to let me know that she fully intended to intimidate me. She leaned in, just six inches from my face, and spat out the words slowly and with intent: "I'm gonna steal you!" I looked back at her, totally unbothered but confused by her posturing, as no actual event led up to her decision to behave this way. Being from South Carolina, I took her words in a literal sense, as the word "steal" did not have any other connotation for me at the time. I shrugged my shoulders, thinking that she was trying to tell me that she was going to somehow steal my purse, which was locked away and concealed from students. Her facial features twitched as my reaction was confusing to her. She leaned in even closer and repeated herself louder, with a deep growl in her voice for emphasis. I started to get the impression that even though what she said made no sense to me, somehow, she definitely wanted to intimidate me, and that my indifferent, puzzled response to her made her quite frustrated. She then gave up and glanced down to the floor. I found out several minutes later that the term "steal" was "to hit or clobber." She was in fact threatening physical harm to me. You see, she saw my demeanor and how I interacted with adults and students, and that seemed foreign to her. She apparently decided to try to intimidate me just to see if I was afraid of her. A scared teacher makes an easy target in the classroom. When I did not show fear nor anger, she was confused. She had not had many interactions with people outside of the community. It was after that incident that I made a concerted effort to listen to the use of words and asked for translation from my colleagues. I also listened and had conversations with students to better understand their realities. By the end of the first week, I had learned a whole new jargon that allowed me to understand students immediately and made my instruction more relevant to their personal experiences.

Lastly, each school has its own culture. Unless you attended that same school with the same leadership, there will be some differences in procedures, priorities, and in-school politics. It is to your benefit to inquire of your mentor and teacher buddy about the ins and outs of school procedures, priorities, and persons of resources within the building. For example, in "School A," there is a designated attendance clerk, book-keeper, nurse, office manager, general secretary, and principal secretary in the main office with specific roles and duties. In "School B," there is one secretary who also plays the roles of attendance clerk, bookkeeper, nurse, and office manager. The main office in "School A" is orderly, and any question that does not pertain to the assigned role of one person is quickly redirected to another. In "School B," the one secretary is always doing seven tasks at once and is short-tempered with everyone. Therefore, if any in-depth question needs to be asked in "School B," veteran teachers and students know to ask elsewhere for the answer. Again, understanding the norms makes your navigation of the school more efficient.

International teachers have the added challenge to acclimate to not only the above issues, but to the culture of the overall country and the particular region and community. **The following are some suggestions to alleviate the culture shock teachers new to the country may experience at any given time during the first school-year experience:**

1) **Self-Care.** Take this major adjustment in stride. Get plenty of sleep, eat well, and stay hydrated to maintain optimal functioning
2) **Keep open lines of communication** with friends and family back home as often and as much as possible.
3) **Challenge yourself to make friends!** Meet faculty members, neighbors, and other people with similar personal interests.
4) **Immerse yourself in the culture!** Attend local and regional cultural events so that you are able to relate to your students' interests.

"Change can be scary, but you know what's scarier? Allowing fear to stop you from Growing, Evolving, and Progressing." ~Mandy Hale

NOTES

Chapter 10:

Expectations for 504 Plans and Individualized Education Plans (IEP)

All teachers within public schools interact with and instruct diversified student populations. One of the areas of diversities involves physical, emotional, and learning abilities. As the general community becomes aware of medical and educational resources, K-12 students with disabilities or challenges are becoming less likely to matriculate through public schools without being properly diagnosed and made aware of the resources to assist the student in having a successful learning experience. For students who may be at a significant disadvantage in a regular classroom setting due to physical, emotional, and/or learning challenges, there may be a 504 Plan or individualized education plan (IEP), which are created by the school psychologist, an administrator, guidance counselor, regular and special education teachers, for the students affected and their parents or guardians.

A 504 Plan is created primarily for students with temporary situations that may need accommodations for a specified period of time. One example of a temporary situation is that a student may have broken or lost glasses, which will not be replaced for two weeks. Therefore, the student may need priority seating on the front row or close to the SMART Board, with permission to stand and move closer, if necessary. Another example of a temporary situation is that a student is under a doctor's care and must take medication for approximately a month or two that may require frequent restroom visits. Once the temporary situation ceases, the 504 Plan is dissolved and the teacher is no longer required to provide the accommodations for that student.

With an IEP, each of the affected students and the designated team of adults are tasked with the responsibility of creating a long term, customized, legal document, which includes the diagnosis, behavioral or cognitive challenges, and list of accommodations. This legal documentation is usually crafted in the spring semester of the school year and is revisited and adjusted annually or whenever adjustments are required, as recommended by one or more of the members of the IEP team. Each member of the team signs the legal document, and all teachers of the student involved are required to strictly follow the accommodations outlined as applicable to their classroom. One example of a situation that requires an IEP is when a student has been formally diagnosed with ADHD and is under a doctor's care; they may or may not be taking prescriptions but need the teacher to provide verbal cues to redirect him/her, behavioral time-outs, and/or weekly emails or documentation to update the counselor or parent/guardian on behavioral or academic progress.

As a teacher, you will be required to attend 504 and IEP meetings when called upon. Typically, these meetings occur before school, during your planning period, or after school. If you are pulled for a meeting during class time, administrators are required to provide classroom supervision while you are away. The length of these meetings vary according to the topics needing to be discussed and the promptness of arrival of everyone involved. Typically, most meetings last for ten to thirty minutes, but an hour-long meeting is not unheard of in extreme circumstances.

At the very beginning of the school year, typically by the end of the first week of school, all teachers should be given a copy of the 504 Plan or IEP for each student with accommodations.

Here are some important points to remember about 504s and IEPs:

1. It is of the utmost importance to create a file folder or notebook where you can keep this confidential information in an accessible but off-limits area within your desk area and away from the eyes of those who may approach your teacher desk for any length of time.
2. Read each 504 Plan or IEP thoroughly. You are legally required to fulfill each of the listed accommodations. Stating that you were not aware or did not know is considered unprofessional and does not release you from your legal obligation.
3. Make sure that you cultivate classroom policies that include these accommodations in a manner that does not single out the student with the IEP directly. For example, many middle or high school students with IEPs require extra time to take tests. Therefore, make it a class policy to have "Test Day," where students have the entire class period to work on the test, with enrichment assignments for those who finish early. This should eliminate the need for most students, with or without an IEP, to need extra testing time. However, in the rare case that a student with an IEP is working consistently for the entire class period and still needs time, you are still required to provide that extra time. Just be sure to provide extra time discreetly (i.e., before or after school, etc.).

"Giving people self-confidence is by far the most important thing that I can do. Because then they will act."
~Jack Welch

NOTES

Chapter 11:

Walk-Throughs, Informal Observations, & Formal Classroom Observations

Being a professional educator includes the necessity to ensure that teachers are giving effective instruction and following the curriculum in a timely manner in each classroom. This is done through both informal and formal observations and evaluations by school administrators. Teachers are often invited to participate in more casual group peer observations (learning walks/walk-throughs) for the purpose of professional growth and the building of school culture in instructional methods. In this chapter, we will explore the most important things for teachers to prepare their classrooms, lesson plans, and instructional methods in a manner that creates class procedure norms for both you as the teacher and for students and that showcase the type of learning environment that is needed to align with the school mission and improve standardized test scores. Reviewing your classroom set-up and decoration decisions in chapter two should prepare you for any observation or evaluation throughout the school year.

Let's take a look at "look-fors" that may occur during random visits by the administrative team or during learning walks first. Whenever administrators or a group of colleagues stop in your classroom, the following are **"Look for"** elements that are listed on their checklist:

1) **Classroom rules/consequences** are prominently displayed in the classroom.

2) **Lesson objective, curriculum standard, or essential question–** This "look for" may vary from school to school. Your administrator should explicitly state what should be displayed each day for students to readily view.

3) **Content-related and skill posters/decor**

4) **Student work displayed with teacher feedback**

5) **Capacity for individual and small group collaborations**

6) **Location of the teacher's desk** allows for student access and proximity to the classroom door.

7) **Evidence that students understand and follow classroom procedures and expectations.**

The **"Listen-fors"** for administrator visits and learning walks include the following:

1) **Clear and explicit directions** that are repeated at least once by teacher

2) **Teacher adjustment to needs of students** (i.e., adjust lights, seating, re-teach, offer additional examples)

3) **Questions asked of students that model higher-order thinking**

4) **Evidence of schema building and higher-order thinking by individual students** and collaborating students (review Bloom's Taxonomy)

5) **Lesson Closure**

Informal and formal observations are typically completed by either the principal, an assistant principal, or a district employee who has officially been trained and authorized to conduct teacher evaluations (i.e., instructional coordinators, etc.). The primary difference between informal and formal observations is that informal observations may or may not be announced, whereas formal observations are typically announced. In the case of an informal observation, an administrator may randomly stop by your classroom and spend fifteen minutes or up to the entire class period with your class at least twice during the first school year. The administrator may occasionally interact with students during small group or individual work time to determine if they are aware of the lesson's objective and their understanding of the expectations, comprehension, and knowledge of class procedures. Spending the first few days of the school year reviewing class procedures, expectations, and daily reminders pays off well, making these habits second nature for your students when it's time for observations. Typically, the administrator will share feedback with you verbally and in electronic or paper form. You can expect the feedback to be rather brief, including some positive feedback, as well as a suggestion or two for "look-fors" or "listen-fors" that were not witnessed or could be enhanced.

Formal observations are more structured, announced, and involve both a pre- and post-observation conference. An administrator should contact you to schedule your formal observation, typically between October and February of the school year. An administrator will contact you for a pre-observation conference, during which you may be allowed to choose the class period and time for the observation. In other cases, the administrator may inquire about your most challenging class, discuss your progress with instruction and/or classroom management, and observe that particular class in order to offer you support with objective feedback.

Formal observations should be viewed as a collaborative opportunity with administrators and as an opportunity to grow professionally. Know that it is not unusual for administrators to learn new instructional strategies and effective classroom management techniques from teachers during these observations! So relax and do your best, as this is all a part of building a strong professional learning community within your school. Administrators are observing how well you adjust and adapt to whatever mishaps (i.e., Johnny trips and falls, Rene begins singing, etc.) occurs. If Johnny falls and the class erupts into laughter, stay calm, make sure that Johnny is okay, then quiet the class down with the sense that you are still in control of the class environment. Most students will follow the lead of your tone of voice and body language. Again, the first few days and weeks of the school year are critical in establishing this rapport and class norm so that students are much less likely to deviate from this norm during observations.

Administrators should remain for most, if not all, of the total class period to observe for the formal observation. Most administrators will bring a tablet or laptop to fill in at least some of the documentation that they are required to complete. This documentation will be shared with you and discussed in detail during the post-observation conference. Again, the focus is to empower the teacher to feel ownership of their classroom learning environment and support them by offering both positive feedback and suggestions for improvement in instructional strategies and classroom management. You will have the opportunity to ask questions, ask for resources, and for any professional development and support that you need in the future.

"Education is not preparation for life; education is life itself."
~John Dewey

NOTES

Chapter 12:

Wrapping Up –
End of the Year Procedures

The first year of teaching will forever remain in your memory! All of the beginning of the year excitement and anticipation, the first angst of mental exhaustion in October, the rigors of fall activities and deadlines, the reminiscence of the holidays, the first breath of fresh air at the beginning of the second semester, and now here you are, enjoying the fruits of your labor in the spring. At this point, your students are well acclimated to your classroom, and you have been enjoying a definite rhythm to the learning process for a few months now. If you are like many new teachers, during this time of the school year, your sights are set on the last day of school.

Here are a few tips and reminders as you wind down during the last couple months of the school year:

1) **"Spring fever."** Stay consistent with classroom management until the last day of school. "spring fever" is real in regard to student behavior from Pre-K to twelfth grade and can and will become a behavioral tsunami if you relax your expectations.

2) **Standardized testing.** Attend training and ask questions of your testing coordinator or guidance counselor. Follow all testing rules and do not deviate, as doing so may have legal consequences.

3) **Parent/Guardian contacts.** Be sure to notify parents and guardians of students who are in danger of failing the quarter and/or the course (D average or below) four weeks before the end of the year via email or mailed letter. This applies even if you have conducted previous conferences and phone calls in the weeks prior.

4) **Gather all technology and accessories**. Notify the technology coordinator or media center specialist if you are missing equipment.

5) **End of year check out.** Most principals send an electronic or paper checklist for end of year check out for faculty and staff. Some schools require that teachers remove all decor from the walls and label furniture for summer cleaning. Some schools only require you to clean and clear your room only if you are not returning the next year. Seek clarity on this expectation.

6) **Summer professional development.** Consider opportunities for professional development during the summer and register for them if applicable.

7) **Grading assignments.** Work daily to grade all assignments and return them to students in a timely manner. Avoid assigning detailed projects or lengthy essays that are due during the last week of school. The timely verification and printing of report cards in most public schools are contingent upon all teachers submitting their final grades without any mistakes.

8) **Be positive and patient.** With the anticipation of summer, even faculty members can be a little anxious to begin their summer. So smile and enjoy the last moments of the faculty social events as the report cards are printed and are being finalized.

9) **Congratulations on a successful first year and enjoy your summer!**

"Success is the sum of small efforts, repeated day in and day out."
~Robert Collier

NOTES

Chapter 13:

Professional Organizations

As an aspiring or certified teacher, building your professional development through organizations is a phenomenal way to expand your professional network and to be exposed to innovative thinking along your professional journey. Professional organizations within the career of education can be categorized as either grade level (i.e., elementary or secondary level), national organizations, state level associations, subject or course area organizations, or "other" professional organizations that cover specialized areas not included in the previous categories.

Examples of Grade Level Professional Organizations
*Note: These examples are not an inclusive list of all of the grade level professional organizations.

Early Childhood Learning & Knowledge Center – This organization provides educators with information and various resources on school readiness, policy, and professional training.

National Middle School Association – This organization is dedicated solely to the middle school grade levels and offers professional development opportunities, educational research, research journals, and professional books for middle school educators.

Examples of National Associations

As the category title suggests, these collective groups disperse valuable information, professional opportunities, benefits, and advocacy methods for teachers across the nation through active recruitment and membership. **Below are just two examples of such organizations but by no means exhaust the list.**

American Federation of Teachers – This organization is a labor union of educational professionals that focuses on democracy, high-quality educational environments, and fair social and economic opportunities. These ideals are achieved through community engagement, organization, collective bargaining, and political activism. This organization is supported by state and local level memberships.

National Education Association – This organization is also a labor union, whose focus is to advocate for education professionals and to unite association members and the nation to fulfill the promise of public education in preparing highly educated and competitive learners for the global society. This organization is also supported by state and local level memberships.

Examples of Subject Area Organizations
Note: These examples are not an inclusive list of all of the subject area organizations.

American International English Teacher Association (www.americanenglish.co) – This association caters to providing curriculum resources for English teachers, as well as covering professional opportunities, such as teaching abroad, teaching online, or tutoring opportunities.

Association of Mathematics Teachers Educators (www.amte.net) – This association supports math teachers in providing curriculum resources, professional development opportunities, and advocacy of resources extended to various minority student groups.

Association for Science Teacher Education (www.theaste.org) – This association caters to providing curriculum resources for science teachers, as well as covering professional development opportunities.

Music Teachers National Association (www.mtna.org) – This association supports music teachers (choral, band, orchestra, etc.) in providing professional seminars, business resources, networking, and membership benefits.

National Art Teacher Association (www.arteducators.org) – This association provides advocacy of social and economic issues, professional development opportunities, events, and membership benefits.

National Association of Special Education Teachers (www.naset.org) – This association provides research publications, membership benefits, and professional development opportunities.

National Council for the Social Studies (www.ncss.org) – This association provides professional development opportunities and curriculum resources for social studies teachers.

Other Professional Organizations

There are several areas of professional advancement or specialization to consider for your professional long-term goals.

American School Counselor Association (www.schoolcounselor.org)

National Association of School Psychologists (www.nasponline.org)

American Association of School Administrators (www.aasa.org)

"Knowledge will bring you the opportunity to make a difference."
~Claire Fagin

Highly Recommended Professional Books

The First Days of School: How to be an effective teacher by Harry K. Wong & Rosemary T. Wong

Who Moved My Cheese? By Spencer Johnson, M.D.

The Novice Advantage: Fearless practice for every teacher by Jonathan Eckert

Learning and Leading with Habits of Mind: 16 essential characteristics for success by Arthur L. Costa & Bena Kallick

Why Don't Students Like School? Second Edition by Daniel T. Willingham

Project Based Learning: Real questions, real answers by Ross Cooper and Erin Murphy

Hacking Engagement Again: This will make students love your class by James Alan Sturtevant

Invent to Learn: Making, tinkering, and engineering in the classroom by Sylvia Libow Martinez & Gary Stager, M.D.

CPSIA information can be obtained
at www.ICGtesting.com
Printed in the USA
LVHW020733170323
741830LV00008B/460